Focus on You:
Your Needs Matter Too!

ALSO BY MICHAEL WOULAS, Ph.D.

The Ticking Time Bomb:

Anger, Rage and Emotional Volatility of Bipolar Disorder Type II

ALSO BY APRIL O'LEARY, B.A.

Ride the Wave:

Journey to Peaceful Living

Focus on You:
Your Needs Matter, Too!

6 Simple Lessons to Help You
Take Better Care of You

Michael Woulas, Ph.D. and

April O'Leary, B.A.

This course is designed to provide accurate and authoritative information in regard to the subject matter covered, and every effort has been made to ensure that it is correct and complete. However, neither the publisher nor the authors are engaged in rendering professional advice or services to the individual reader, and this book is not intended as a substitute for advice from a trained counselor, therapist, coach or other similar professional. If you require such advice or other expert assistance, you should seek the services of a competent professional in the appropriate specialty.

This book is available at a special quantity discount for bulk purchase for sales promotions, premiums, fund-raising, and educational needs. Special excerpts also can be created for specific needs. For details please write to ILM Publishing, 28089 Vanderbilt Drive, Suite 202, Bonita Springs, FL 34134.

First Paperback Edition 2012

Cover Design by Christine Dupre
Editing by Jennifer Freihoefer

ISBN-13:978-1478273028
ISBN-10:147827302X

Printed in the United States of America

Table of Contents

Introduction   1

Lesson 1: What Is Codependency?   2

Lesson 2: It's Not Selfish to Take Care of You!   14

Lesson 3: Overcoming Fear and Guilt   28

Lesson 4: Overcoming Fear and Guilt – A Personal Story   42

Lesson 5: Other Causes of Codependency   56

Lesson 6: Happiness Begins with You   68

Conclusion   80

About the Authors   85

Appendix I - Research Initiative   87

Appendix II- 3 Month Follow-Up   89

Notes   93

Introduction

Welcome to the first course in the *Focus on You* series. <u>Focus on You: Your Needs Matter Too</u> has been designed to help you to create more balance in your life. Each lesson will take you through a process of recognizing and improving your abilities to effectively take care of yourself even while in the midst of caring for others.

TO SIGN UP FOR FREE WEEKLY LESSON REMINDERS AND AUDIO FILES GO TO: www.instituteforlifemanagement.com/level1audios

---

Do you usually find it difficult to confront others with what you really want to do? Do you have a hard time saying 'no' to others? Are you angry or frustrated because there seems to be so little time for you? If you answered 'yes' to any of these questions, then you will benefit from the *Focus on You* series.

It is very important to put time and effort into answering all the questions provided, in writing. They have been specifically designed to take you to a higher level of awareness and interpersonal development. There is also a section for Notes at the back of the workbook.

At the completion of this course you can expect to:

- Achieve a greater understanding of codependency and the variety of ways in which it can occur.
- Become more aware of healthy and unhealthy relationship patterns.
- Learn where fear and guilt originate and how to effectively deal with them.
- Acquire a higher level of personal satisfaction in your relationships.

In addition to participating in the course you are encouraged to visit our websites for further resources and help. Remember, your needs matter, too.

Michael Woulas, Ph.D., Psychotherapist
hereishelp.net
instituteforlifemanagement.com

April O'Leary, B.A., Life Coach
apriloleary.com
uofmoms.com

Lesson 1:

What Is Codependency?

Lesson 1 Overview

In this lesson you will learn that codependent personality traits are very common in our world today. Most people struggle with some of these characteristics, but you will see that codependency is allowing yourself to focus too much on the needs of others and ignoring your own needs in the process. Keep in mind that fear is at the root of most of these patterns.

We hope that through the self-assessment at the end of this lesson you will become aware of the specific personality traits that make it difficult for you to take care of your own emotional needs. Through this awareness you will start the process of change, during which you will find that meeting your own needs matters, too.

Please answer the following questions before starting Lesson 1 to assess your own knowledge:

1. Write your own definition of codependency.

2. Do you see yourself as a codependent person? Why or why not?

3. What problems are you facing right now in your relationships that you hope to resolve?

Lesson 1

What Is Codependency?

April O'Leary:

Welcome to *Focus on You*. This is a six-lesson series to help you take care of you. I am April O'Leary, life coach and author of <u>Ride the Wave: Journey to Peaceful Living</u> and I am here with Dr. Michael Woulas, psychotherapist and author of the book <u>The Ticking Time Bomb.</u>

Welcome, Dr. Woulas.

Dr. Michael Woulas:

Thank you April. I am looking forward to this six-lesson series.

April O'Leary:

Yes. I think it will be very informative. As a brief overview, throughout this series we'll be covering topics ranging from self-care, to releasing the need to please others, to overcoming fear and guilt and I'll even be sharing a personal story of how I overcame guilt in my own life and we'll conclude with a very important topic, and one of my favorites, creating happiness. So let's get started with Lesson 1: What is Codependency? Would you like to tell us, Dr. Woulas, what is codependency?

Dr. Michael Woulas:

Sure. Codependency, April, is a term that has been around for many, many years. Initially, codependency was associated primarily with spouses or partners of people who suffer from addictions of one form or another.

April O'Leary:

And has that definition of codependency evolved since then?

4

Dr. Michael Woulas: Yes, generally in behavioral health today, many practitioners, including myself, are using the term codependency as a term that includes many unhealthy personality traits that can be targeted and focused on as a person goes through therapy.

April O'Leary: What kind of personality traits are you referring to?

Dr. Michael Woulas: One of the primary personality traits that we would consider to be codependent is a person's need to focus most of their attention and time on a significant other, rather than themselves. So, as they do this, they are basically saying that the significant other, who they are focusing their attention, time and efforts on, would be considered, by that person, much more important than themselves.

April O'Leary: Are you saying that it is unhealthy to take care of someone before yourself?

Dr. Michael Woulas: Well, basically, when you talk about codependency we are talking about extremes of personality traits like focusing too much on others and not enough on yourself. In other words, there is really nothing inappropriate or unhealthy about caring for others and focusing on their needs and interest, to a point, but when you look at people who do this excessively you see that they are unable to balance things. In others words, it becomes very difficult for them to put enough time and effort into themselves. So, it's a question of degree.

April O'Leary: Yes. And that's why we are here, to talk about getting the focus off of someone else and putting it back on to you. So, how common is codependency? Is it something you see on a regular basis?

Dr. Michael Woulas:	Yes. I believe today, April, it's very, very common, and I think over time it has become increasingly more common. Think of it in terms of the problem of addiction. In the past, codependency was associated with a spouse of somebody who suffers from addiction. Over time, especially over the past several decades, there has been an incredible increase in the amount of people who suffer from addictions of various kinds. So, for every person that suffers from some form of addiction you can almost be certain that they have a spouse or a partner who has been affected by their disease, and they are the ones that develop codependent personality traits. So, it's been prevalent as long as addictions have been on the planet, and as the problem of addiction tends to escalate, so does codependency.
April O'Leary:	Is it possible someone could struggle with codependency or codependent patterns if their spouse or significant other doesn't have an addiction such as alcoholism or another specific drug problem?
Dr. Michael Woulas:	Yes. Most people think of addiction in terms of drugs or alcohol, but 'addiction' is just another term for dependency. People can become overly dependent or addicted to many things besides drugs and alcohol. For example, work can be a source of addiction for a lot of people. Food can also become an addiction as well.
April O'Leary:	If someone has a spouse who is addicted to work, could that person also suffer from codependent patterns?
Dr. Michael Woulas:	Yes. The spouse or partner, April, of the person who has an addiction or dependency on work would be the one who becomes codependent. Now, we probably need to talk a little bit more about what those traits are. I think I have described codependency generally as the tendency to be overly focused or overly dependent on another person or another thing, but there are several other traits that also go along with codependency.

6

April O'Leary:	Can you make a list of what those traits are so we can get a big picture?
Dr. Michael Woulas:	Sure. One core emotion that seems to underlie most people with codependency is fear or anxiety.
April O'Leary:	So, is it fear or anxiety towards their partner or fear or anxiety in general?
Dr. Michael Woulas:	I would say both of those. But a person who we call codependent usually suffers from a lot of fear and anxiety, and it's usually not fear or anxiety of any specific thing. It's not like having a specific phobia. It's generally being fearful and anxious.
April O'Leary:	Could you give me an example of the workaholic husband and how the wife might be exhibiting codependent patterns of anxiety?
Dr. Michael Woulas:	One of the primary fears in codependency is the fear of being rejected. For example, the workaholic would not spend enough time at home or in the relationship and pretty much send a message to the partner that they are not that important. That would be one type of rejection.
April O'Leary:	So, in what way does she compensate for that in the relationship or in her own personality that would be codependent?
Dr. Michael Woulas:	That's a very good question. This is something that happens on a regular basis in codependency, where the codependent partner would be making very serious attempts at gaining her

husband's attention. So, for example, the codependent partner may try to arrange for special times together, may go out of his or her way to buy things for that person to get their attention, to prepare foods that they like and basically become what we might call 'a people pleaser,' all in an effort to get the love and attention from the partner.

April O'Leary: That's very eye opening, I am sure, for a lot of listeners. There is a difference between meeting someone's needs in a healthy way versus doing something in order to get attention because of the underlying fear of rejection.

Dr. Michael Woulas: Exactly. Fear or anxiety, which is basically the same thing, underlies most of the codependent personality. Fear underlies and directs most of their actions, and it's basically fear of not being loved.

April O'Leary: Okay. So for our listeners benefit can you tell us: How does someone know if they are codependent? Maybe just hearing this message is causing some fear or anxiety and they might worried that they are putting their spouse first too much or thinking too much of them. How would someone know if they have crossed over into codependent patterns?

Dr. Michael Woulas: You just need to ask yourself a few questions. For example, "Am I spending too much of my time focusing on my spouse or partner and not enough time on myself?" Secondly ask yourself: "Do I seem to experience or suffer from fears or anxiety?" And a third and very important question would be, "How much do you really like yourself, and how important is it for you to receive approval and acceptance from others?" Now, we all like to be accepted to some degree, but again it comes down to question of degree. So, the higher you would rate yourself on those personality characteristics, the closer you are to having crossed that line into codependency.

April O'Leary:
That's a great way to start. Thank you so much. Now it's your turn. Dr. Woulas and I have provided in the following activity a typical codependent self-assessment for you to take. Take ten minutes and go through the statements and see which of them applies to you. The first step is recognizing and becoming aware of unhealthy patterns so be honest as you go through and rate yourself. There are no good or bad answers, this is only for your own personal knowledge. After you are done you may proceed to Lesson 2, where you can expect to hear a little more about the importance of taking care of you. This concludes Lesson 1.

Lesson 1 Activity

Woulas O'Leary Codependent Assessment Scale (WOCAS)

Please rate yourself on a scale from 0-3 for each of the statements below.

0= Not at all
1= Occasionally
2= Frequently
3= All the time

_____ I depend on others for approval and acceptance.

_____ I frequently go out of my way to please others

_____ I find it hard to accept criticism from others.

_____ I focus on the needs of others more than on my own needs.

_____ I would much rather avoid confrontations than speaking my mind.

_____ I notice that my actions are determined by external events.

_____ It seems like my value as a person comes from how well I do in life.

_____ As long as others are happy around me, I'm happy.

_____ If I am honest with myself, I would say I have too much fear.

_____ I have a goal of fixing those whom I am closest with.

_____ As a child I experienced some emotional, physical or sexual abuse.

_____ I have been physically, verbally or sexually assaulted as an adult.

_____ I grew up in a very critical family.

_____ I noticed that my parents were frequently concerned about what others thought.

_____ As a child I was corrected for trying to please myself first.

_____ I remember being called selfish if I didn't put others first all the time.

_____ One or both of my parents tended to be overly negative in their thinking.

_____ If I am honest with myself I have also become too negative in my thinking.

_____ I label others as selfish if they spend time and money on themselves.

_____ Intimacy tends to frighten me.

_____ I find it difficult to accept praise for most of my accomplishments.

_____ I was raised in a family where alcohol and/or drugs were a problem.

_____ I have never really considered the importance of having emotional boundaries.

_____ I find myself frequently making excuses for other peoples' problems.

_____ I generally feel unfulfilled as a person.

_____ There never seems to be enough time for me in a typical day.

_____ People often see me as a 'pushover' or someone who is too easy with others.

_____ There seems to be something wrong with my intimate relationships, but I can't seem to put my finger on it.

_____ I expect people who say they love me to take care of my needs.

_____ One or both of my parents were usually trying to please and make things right with others.

_____ At least one of my grandparents had a history of alcoholism or substance abuse.

_____ One or both of my parents had a bad temper and would lash out at others.

_____ One or both of my parents never seemed to be emotionally available as I was growing up.

_____ My life seems to be passing by and I'm afraid I've missed out on myself.

_____ If I had to do it over again, I would certainly take more time in life for me.

SCORING: Now that you have completed the assessment it's time to tally up your answers. How many of each did you get?

_____ 3's _____ 2's _____ 1's _____ 0's

RESULTS: If you found you scored more 3's and 2's then you have a moderate to severe level of codependency and will benefit greatly from completing this course. If you scored mainly 1's and 0's then you have a mild level of codependency which is typical in most people.

SUMMARY: Taking this course will help you understand the root causes of codependency so that you can more effectively become aware of it in yourself and help others.

Use this checklist as a guide to help identify your potential codependent personality traits. Try to be more aware of the items you have circled on the list because these will be the traits that will make it difficult for you to focus on yourself. Remember, the first step to change is becoming aware. Congratulations on increasing your self-awareness!

Lesson 1 Summary

Codependent personality traits are very common in our world today. Most people struggle with some of these characteristics, but codependency is allowing yourself to focus too much on the needs of others and ignoring your own needs in the process. Keep in mind that fear is at the root of most of these patterns.

We hope that through the self-assessment you have become aware of the specific personality traits that make it difficult for you to take care of your own emotional needs. Through this awareness you have already started the process of change in which meeting your own needs matters, too.

To conclude please write your answers to the following questions:

1. What was most important to you in this lesson? Why?

2. What specific codependent issues have you identified as problematic for you?

3. How do you plan to use this awareness to help create change in your relationships?

Lesson 2:

It's Not Selfish to Take Care of You!

Lesson 2 Overview

In this lesson you will learn that being selfish and taking care of yourself are two entirely different things. We hope that you will learn that it is not selfish to take care of you. The key is to create balance between your needs and the needs of others. It is also important to be aware of and effectively communicate your needs to those around you.

Please write your answers to the following questions before you begin the lesson:

1. List some personality traits of someone you might consider selfish.

2. What are the things they do that appear selfish?

3. What are your thoughts and feelings about people that function this way?

Lesson 2

It's Not Selfish to Take Care of You!

April O'Leary:

This is Lesson 2 of *Focus on You: Your Needs Matter too.* This is April O'Leary and I am here with Dr. Michael Woulas.

In Lesson 1 we shared with you many of the personality traits that stem from codependency. Chances are that after taking the self- assessment, you could identify with a few, if not many, of the statements on the list. Whatever the case it is important to know that overtime, and with some guided instruction, such as this, you can gradually modify those ways of thinking and behaviors that are unhealthy and are causing stress in your relationships and are frustrating you. Today we will focus on general strategies to help you take better care of you.

Welcome, Dr. Woulas.

Dr. Michael Woulas:

Hi, April. Many times when I am seeing patients in the office or talking with people in general, the conversation of self-care may come up. But, when I allude to the fact that it's important to focus on yourself, I sometimes get a funny look.

April O'Leary:

I can see where that might confuse people. Most of us are taught that it is more important to meet everyone else's needs first.

Dr. Michael Woulas:

If you ask someone what they think about focusing on yourself, you might hear objections like, "Isn't that being selfish?" or "I was never raised to think about me." I know this is a very important part of your work and what you are trying to accomplish, April, isn't it?

16

April O'Leary:	For sure! I coach people in many areas of self-care and help them realize that it's not selfish to take care of yourself first. Now, I will admit that I was guilty of putting everyone else first for years when my children were younger which caused me a lot of needless stress, and it was at that time that I came to realize that it doesn't work.
Dr. Michael Woulas:	How did you come to realize, April, that putting other people first doesn't really work?
April O'Leary:	Well as women we are often taught that putting others first is our job. Whether we got that message through our culture, our religion, or through mass marketing, women are taught to be the care-takers of everyone. Because of this, like many women I know, I never considered putting myself first or even making my needs a priority. So, when I had children I did what I saw all around me...I started taking care of everyone else. But your question was, how did I realize that didn't work? The answer is I started getting resentful and angry. I started snapping at the kids, and my generally happy and good-natured personality vaporized into thin air and I couldn't figure out why.
Dr. Michael Woulas:	It's true that people can get the message that putting others first is the right way to do things through religion, by watching other people, through cultural tradition and even through advertising. So, it sounds like you basically began putting other people ahead of you as a result of many of these things.
April O'Leary:	Yes and I did so unknowingly. There is a common misconception that it's most appropriate to put others first and then you. You are always secondary. If you are at all religious, you might find you were taught to put God first, then others, and then you. So now you have moved yourself down to third place. It's no wonder we never have time for

ourselves if we think this way. Without really realizing it that's how I was living my life. I was consistently putting everyone else first and thinking, "When there is time I will get to me." or "If I have enough energy left I will get to me." Somehow that time and that energy was never available, and so all these 'others' that I was focusing on, started to become the source of my anger.

Dr. Michael Woulas: So that is one of the ways you realized, April, that putting way too much attention on others really wasn't working for you.

April O'Leary: It was. Previous to having children, I was typically a happy and funny person, at least I like to think so, and the way I had changed through the stress of motherhood was alarming. It was 'unlike' me to be snapping and angry and resentful. So I knew something wasn't right and I decided to get some help. My counselor, at the time, gave me the same information that we are sharing with you today in this program. I learned that it was not selfish to take care of me, although I certainly struggled with that concept at the time. I remember saying that I would feel selfish and thinking that wasn't right, but I was smart enough to realize that what I was doing wasn't' working because of the way I was generally feeling.

Dr. Michael Woulas: So, in a sense, it took you to the point of where you were not feeling very well emotionally, and you needed to get a better understanding of what was going on, and that's when it was pointed out to you that you were feeling the way you were because you were not taking enough time for yourself.

April O'Leary: That is exactly right. I couldn't have said it better myself. It was a process. When you are used to putting all your desires and needs on the back burner and not thinking about them at all, it can feel quite scary and uncomfortable to start changing that. I can remember back then that if I was asked where I would like to go to dinner, my response might have been, "I don't know. Where do you want to go?" I know that is a basic example, but it shows that I was always thinking, "What does everyone else want?" I was more concerned with everyone else's opinions, desires, thoughts and I didn't want to upset anyone. I just wanted to make everybody happy.

Dr. Michael Woulas: When it was pointed out to you that it's okay to meet others' needs to a point but that you would probably feel better emotionally if you started to focus a little bit more on yourself, you felt unsure about that. Is that right?

April O'Leary: I did. I can remember feeling resentful towards a few other women I knew who were taking good care of themselves. The thoughts that consistently caused me anger towards them were telling me that they have no idea what my life is like. I also thought of my life as harder or less-manageable and honestly thought that I could never get a day to myself. Of course, having three young children, it does require a bit of planning to meet your needs, but I was trapped with all of these thoughts, that led me to believe that it wasn't possible to take care of myself, and secondly, that a good mother would set aside herself for her children, like I was doing. When you do this, however, you not only become resentful of your family, but it's hard to be happy for other people, who are taking the steps they need to take care of themselves, too.

So, back then I got stuck in this cycle of negativity not realizing that I was not taking care of myself. Also, since I was spending so much of my time taking care of everyone else, I was expecting somebody else to do that for me, and when that didn't happen, the resentfulness started to build in my relationships with others.

Dr. Michael Woulas: Would you say that, from your experience, this is a very common issue with most wives and mothers out there today?

April O'Leary:	Yes I would. I know that men can also struggle with these patterns too, but I would say based on my own experience, the reason I lived this way for so long was that I didn't really know anyone else who was doing anything different. I think that most of the women I knew, who were at-home or working, were also meeting others needs ahead of their own. Typically women get together and complain about how hard they work, how unappreciated they are, and how they never get any time for themselves, and that seems normal. After the conversation is over they feel better because they think, although this stinks, this is normal. "Everyone else is in the same boat, so this must be the way it is."
Dr. Michael Woulas:	So, from your experience, it sounds like it is a very common issue for many people.
April O'Leary:	It is. Thankfully, you can make a choice not to live this way anymore and take steps to make some corrections in your thinking and in the way you interact in your relationships with others. It is very important to know yourself, to know what you like, to make time for yourself and to put yourself back on the priority list. The more you do this, the more you will be able to enjoy your life and not be so angry and resentful.
Dr. Michael Woulas:	Do you think you can give some specific examples now about what it means, April, to take care of yourself?
April O'Leary:	Sure. That's a great question, and it's really specific for each person. There are a few questions you might ask yourself. The first is, "How much time do I need for myself on a daily, weekly and monthly basis?" There are no wrong or right answers to this question and there is nothing to feel guilty about. Taking time for yourself and focusing on your needs will make you a more relaxed, happier individual overall. So, if you need a whole day to yourself once a month, that's a perfectly normal and healthy idea. It's realistic and reasonable

to want to have an hour or two to yourself each day. You really have to be in touch with your own needs, and then take steps to figure out a way to meet those needs yourself. That might mean setting boundaries and saying 'no' to some of the activities you have committed to. Whether you are volunteering too often, working too much or meeting other's needs before your own regularly, it is possible to finally say 'no', and acknowledge that you can't do it all and then set boundaries for yourself. Although it takes a little time and requires you take some action, I have found that setting boundaries is an effective way of showing that you are starting to take care of you, by not putting everyone else first. The more we say 'yes' to others needs above our own and the more we over-commit ourselves, the more we are showing ourselves that everyone else is the priority. But by setting boundaries and making our needs a priority we can alleviate a lot of the built up anger and resentment that comes from living this way. Setting boundaries is definitely the healthier option.

Dr. Michael Woulas: That sounds like really good advice, April. I think the things that you are describing right here are helpful. Taking time for yourself is very important, isn't it?

April O'Leary: It is critical.

Dr. Michael Woulas: Setting boundaries is a good idea too.

April O'Leary: Yes. Setting boundaries is a big one, and it's often difficult because of the fear of rejection. You may fear that the people who asked you to participate in their organization or on their committee might reject you if you don't say 'yes' to what they are asking.

Dr. Michael Woulas: So, setting boundaries is a very important step to take when you are trying to take care of yourself.

April O'Leary: One tip that I'd like to share with those of us who are used to saying 'yes' and who struggle with slowing down and setting boundaries is to "never say yes on the spot." That's an easy rule to live by. If someone asks you to do something, always give yourself some time to think first. You might say, "Thank you for the offer. Let me look at my calendar, and I will get back with you." I was as guilty of this as anybody, especially when my kids were little. I felt like I needed to commit to every last activity, and I was exhausted and resentful.

Dr. Michael Woulas: There are some pretty slick people out there who are always trying to recruit others for their time and resources. They know that if they confront somebody and put them on the spot they are likely to commit. It's a very common thing for women, when they are put on the spot like that, to want to say 'yes,' because if they say 'no', they think they are doing something wrong.

April O'Leary: It is definitely a big one. There are so many opportunities to volunteer, and to get involved in groups these days, and they are always looking for volunteers. When you start using this strategy of 'never saying 'yes' on the spot' it can feel uncomfortable, but the time you give yourself to think about it is well spent.

Dr. Michael Woulas: But what if someone is already over-committed? What would you suggest they do?

April O'Leary: I was taught that if you commit to something you have to follow through and do it. Now although this is helpful, it can be taken too far. Some commitments will never end unless you put an end to them and if you no longer enjoy participating or it is taking too much of your time you might have to consider ending the commitment. If you have already said 'yes' and you want to start setting boundaries so you can reclaim a little time for yourself I would like you to remember that just because you have done something once doesn't mean you need to continue doing it. So, just because you volunteered last year doesn't mean that you have to continue doing that this year. You can decide to start setting your boundaries and start saying 'no,' and you'll soon realize that your contribution, although kind, was not irreplaceable. Someone else will take that position, as much as they would like you to believe that they can't survive without you. Somebody else will say 'yes.'

Dr. Michael Woulas: Right. Then there is nothing wrong with that, is there?

April O'Leary: No, no. It's actually very freeing. When you start clearing off your calendar, and realize you have a little more time for yourself, to replenish your energy reserves, you'll feel better, which in turn makes you a better person overall. It's a good feeling.

Dr. Michael Woulas: Then it gets back to what you said initially about being unable to take time for yourself. You have to have a schedule that allows you to take time.

April O'Leary: For most of us, the reason we don't have the time is because we've over-committed ourselves. If you think, "There is no way I can get a day to myself", "I just don't have time" or "It's impossible," it's not because it's truly impossible, it's because you have made the choice to over-commit yourself. You have simply said 'yes' to too many things. You have to start looking at your calendar objectively to determine what is reasonable to eliminate. You might see that with a little practice eliminating things becomes easier and easier. I would say that now it's harder to get me to commit to something than it is to get me to say 'no' to something.

Dr. Michael Woulas: Well, that's progress.

April O'Leary: It really is.

Dr. Michael Woulas: What side of the fence do you think you want to be on?

April O'Leary: I think it's easier to say 'no.' Since we are talking about the practical 'how to' aspect of taking care of you, if you say 'no' initially and then you decide a week or two later that you really would like to say 'yes,' chances are that door will still be open. They are always looking for volunteers, always looking for people to chair committees and be on boards. So, if you say 'no' and then you decide, "Ah, I think I missed the opportunity," make the phone call, and I am sure they will still gladly accept you.

Dr. Michael Woulas: Well, April, I think that is a good start. We've covered a few of the important issues that have to do with taking care of yourself, and the specific things you can do to take care of yourself. Always remember that when you do that, it's not being selfish.

April O'Leary: That's right, Dr. Woulas. Now it's your turn. Go ahead and complete the Lesson 2 activity. Remember to take your time with the activities as this is where the real work starts. If you are struggling with correcting your thinking about meeting your own needs first, remember that the more you take action to change what is not working the more you will see the results and you'll be convinced that this works. All it takes is little adjustments, over time. Thank you for listening in and this concludes Lesson 2.

Lesson 2 Activity

Is It Selfish?

Answer the following questions by deciding whether you feel the statement is selfish or not. Circle 'yes' to signify that it IS selfish. Circle 'no' if it is NOT selfish.

- Brenda wants to go out to a movie with her friends. It's a 6:00 show, so she would miss dinner at home. YES NO

- Sarah is tired and asks her husband to watch the kids so she can take a nap. He has worked all week, too. YES NO

- Dawn says 'no' when she is asked to chair the membership committee. They really do need some help. YES NO

- Grace decides to take her children out of swimming because the nightly practices are too time consuming. The coach is disappointed. YES NO

- Andrew says 'no' to working on a Saturday morning because he had planned to golf. He wonders if he should have gone in. YES NO

- Monica declines an invitation to go to a cookware party her friend is hosting. She doesn't ask for the catalog to order anything, either. YES NO

- Maria doesn't answer her phone when she is cooking dinner even though it is her sister. She feels a bit guilty. YES NO

- After joining the school P.T.O. Emily realizes she just doesn't have the time. She backs out. The other women are a bit annoyed and disappointed. YES NO

- Kelly loves scrapbooking. She has quite a collection of materials that she has bought from a specialty shop. One Saturday a month her husband watches the kids so she can spend the entire day with friends working on her scrapbooks. YES NO

- Mallory hires a cleaning lady because she hates cleaning the house and finds she doesn't have the time, even though she is home with her young children. YES NO

- Linda orders meals from a local chef who has a home-delivery service so she doesn't have to cook. YES NO

What did you answer? All of them are 'no.' Does that surprise you? It is hard to classify someone as 'selfish' if they are simply doing what they NEED to do. But it is not selfish to do what you WANT to do. That is why setting your boundaries and knowing yourself are both so critical. It is also important to strike a balance. You must consider others while meeting your own needs, which requires communication, too. Go ahead and do what you want to do and what you need to do: to take care of you! It's not selfish!

List 3 things below that you would like to do but have not done because you thought it was selfish. Do they still seem selfish?

1)

2)

3)

How would you feel if you were able to do them?

What steps can you take to start incorporating these things into your life?

Lesson 2 Summary

Being selfish and taking care of yourself are two entirely different things. We hope that you have learned that it is not selfish to take care of you. Creating balance between your needs and the needs of others is also important and the key to creating balance is awareness and communication.

To conclude please write your answers to the following questions:

1. What was most important to you in this lesson? Why?

2. What things did you formerly think of as being 'selfish' that you now consider necessary in order to take care of you?

3. What do you plan to do this week to make your needs a priority?

Lesson 3:

Overcoming Fear and Guilt

Lesson 3 Overview

In this lesson you will learn where fear and guilt come from and how to recognize it in your own thought patterns. You will see that overcoming fear and guilt may take some time. As you begin to differentiate rational, realistic thinking from irrational and unrealistic thought processes, you will discover how unhealthy fear and guilt occur. By the end of this lesson you will be able to identify illogical thought patterns, which will help alleviate unnecessary fear and guilt.

Before beginning Lesson 3 please answer the following questions:

List one scenario in which you recently felt guilty.

Why did you feel guilty?

Do you feel your guilt was based on realistic perceptions? Why?

Lesson 3

Overcoming Fear and Guilt

April O'Leary: Welcome back. This is April O'Leary, here with Dr. Michael Woulas.

Now that you have a better understanding of codependency and the importance of taking care of you we are going to talk about overcoming unhealthy forms of guilt and fear.

Good afternoon, Dr. Woulas.

Dr. Michael Woulas: Good afternoon, April O'Leary.

April O'Leary: Dr. Woulas is going to provide us with some very insightful information today. So, let start by asking you – where do fear and guilt come from?

Dr. Michael Woulas: Fear and guilt, April, are basic human emotions, and like all human emotions they have their origin in our thinking or in our perceptions of each and every situation that we encounter.

April O'Leary: So, it's the thoughts that we have about our situations that are causing the fear and guilt?

Dr. Michael Woulas: Exactly. And I think this is a very important for our listeners to begin to understand. Most people are not aware that their feelings, like fear and guilt, actually come from their thinking. Most people believe that the way they feel is in direct

30

relationship to the situation that they are experiencing. It is important to become aware that the actual emotion that they experience is the direct result of a thought or perception of the situation.

Before we go into looking at fear and guilt in a little more detail, I think it's very important to understand those concepts.

April O'Leary:
If I am hearing you correctly, what you are saying is, it's not the outside environment that causes fear and guilt, but it's our thoughts about the world around us?

Dr. Michael Woulas:
Exactly, it's our thoughts and our perceptions. So, when anybody experiences fear, for example, they are telling themselves that something bad is about to happen. That is what triggers fear.

For example, imagine you are about to cross a highway on foot. You stop and look both ways before you cross. When you look to your right, you notice that there is a tractor trailer coming down the highway. So, your perception or thought is, "If I step out here at this moment, I am going to get hurt or killed." So, that perception or thought will trigger some fear, which would be healthy. Now, in that situation, the fear is appropriate because your perception is true – there <u>is</u> a truck coming, and if you do step out in front of that truck you are likely to get killed. So, there are times where fear is healthy or appropriate, so to speak.

But oftentimes fear, especially when it involves codependency, is there because of perceptions that are <u>not</u> true.

April O'Leary:	Okay. Unlike the situation you just described – in which the fear you might feel is justified – unhealthy fear is based on something that's not accurate. Would it be like looking down the road and being afraid to cross when there is no truck coming?
Dr. Michael Woulas:	Exactly. You would be standing on the side of the road, looking both ways, and you wouldn't see a thing, but for some reason you would be fearful to cross the road. Now, in that case, fear is coming from a thought which you may not be aware of, and that thought is not true; it is not realistic. You would inaccurately be thinking that something bad is going to happen if you cross the empty road. There is really no reason for you to think those thoughts. Therefore, the fear in that case would be based on a thought that's not realistic.
April O'Leary:	So if I hear you correctly, you are saying that it is realistic to be afraid to cross the road if a truck is coming, and that is healthy fear, but it's not realistic to be afraid to cross an empty road and that is an unhealthy form of fear.
Dr. Michael Woulas:	Exactly. Now, put it in the context of codependency. We discussed in one of the previous lessons that fear tends to be the central, core emotion in codependency and it is a very big inhibitor in terms of action or responses in many situations. If you are afraid to cross a road because a truck is coming, you are telling yourself something that's true, which is that you are going to get hurt. So, you stop and you don't cross the street. Now, in codependency, the fear is unhealthy because it is stemming from untrue thoughts. In the example of the empty road the thoughts would be still alerting the person that they would get hurt crossing the road, which is untrue, but would be preventing them from crossing. It's not an appropriate emotion because it's coming from thoughts and perceptions that are not true or realistic. In other words, unhealthy fear holds the person back unnecessarily, April.

April O'Leary: Can you parallel that with, perhaps, a codependent spouse and the fear that holds them back? How might fear arise in that situation?

Dr. Michael Woulas: Okay. Let's say you are in a codependent relationship with your husband or boyfriend. You get a phone call this afternoon from one of your girl friends who says to you, "April, we have tickets to a show I would like to take you to tonight. Can you come?" and you instantly start to feel frightened. You are feeling frightened because you are saying to yourself, "If I go, something bad may happen to me. Either my husband is going to get mad at me, or my kids may cry, 'Mommy, we want you home. We don't want you to go anywhere.'" So, there is instant fear that if you agree, something bad is going to happen.

Now, the misconception or irrational thought is that, "My kids are not supposed to get upset if I want to leave." Is that realistic? When a parent leaves, most normal children say, "Mommy, don't go. Mommy, we want you home." It's not unrealistic for that to happen. It's also not unusual for husband to not be excited to take care of the children alone for an evening. So if you come in and say, "You know, I have an opportunity to go to this show with so-and-so," it is realistic that he may appear a little disappointed.

Now, both of those external responses are very normal – the husband's as well as the children's – but the codependent wife would see those reactions and be somewhat overcome by fear, which would hold her back from going. She would be overly focused on those responses and say to herself, "Well, if everyone is going to be upset I probably shouldn't go. I shouldn't be getting those kinds of responses." Those thoughts are not realistic.

April O'Leary:	So, by her deciding not to go because her children are saying, "Mommy, we want you at home" or because her husband is tired and doesn't feel like watching the kids alone, that would be equivalent to her looking down the road and perceiving a truck to be there when there is really no truck.
Dr. Michael Woulas:	Exactly. Surely you can see where she is creating fear in that situation when there is really nothing to be afraid of. If she decides to go and her kids say, "Mommy, I don't want you to go," that's a normal thing. That's not a bad thing. That's not a danger.

If her husband seems a little disappointed because she is going to be leaving, and he was expecting her to be there to watch the kids, that's a normal and appropriate response. That's not a bad thing. If she decides to go, that's something he and the children have to deal with. |
April O'Leary:	That makes a lot of sense and I'd like to reiterate – that's something he and the children have to deal with – and it is healthy to put the focus back on you. When the wife is not doing something reasonable, or that she might find enjoyable, because her husband is getting upset, and the kids are saying, "Mommy, mommy, don't go," her focus is on them, it's not on her, and overtime that will make her unhappy.
Dr. Michael Woulas:	Exactly.
April O'Leary:	So, even though she desires to go, she is putting aside the focus on her because of fear based on the responses she is getting, and therefore she is focusing too much on them.
Dr. Michael Woulas:	Fear of the response that she is going to get leads to guilt as well. For people who are overly codependent, they deal with

a lot of fear, and guilt is right there along with it. Guilt, just like fear, comes in situations like these and the guilt is also going to come from a thought or perception that she is doing something wrong.

See, guilt is a normal human emotion. There is nothing wrong with feeling guilt as long as it's coming from a thought that's true or realistic. In other words, guilt comes from a thought that you have done something wrong and it's appropriate to feel guilt if you have done something wrong. But, if you tell yourself you have done something wrong when you really haven't, you are still going to feel guilt, but it's guilt that's unhealthy. It's guilt that's not appropriate to the situation because you really haven't done anything wrong. The key is to be able to become aware when you are feeling guilt based off of a thought you have done something wrong when you really haven't. These are very common thoughts and feelings of people who have a high level of codependency.

| April O'Leary: | So, the fear and guilt that you feel in relation to real dangers or real infractions – like stealing, lying or cheating – are appropriate. However, if you have been offered tickets to go to a show, there is nothing to feel fearful or guilty about because you haven't done anything wrong. |

| Dr. Michael Woulas: | If you go… |

| April O'Leary: | Yes, if you go. So, if someone was offered tickets to a show, it is realistic that they might want to go to it. When that person can put the focus back on themselves a little and say, "Yes, I want to go to this show," then they have to let go of the idea that they can control everyone else's responses. That would be focusing on others. |

Dr. Michael Woulas: Correct.

April O'Leary: It's okay if the husband is upset and the kids are crying when she leaves. It's really not within her control to change that.

Dr. Michael Woulas: True, but let's not leave out, the importance of communication as well. In other words, waiting until the husband comes home to actually tell him this is probably not the best thing to do. The more appropriate thing would be to call him at work or leave a message and let him know what's going on. If you make a decision that you want to go, then go ahead and tell the children. You could even delay the decision until you get a chance to talk to your husband to see if maybe there was something special that came up with him that he hadn't had a chance to talk with you about, or same thing with the kids. Communication is always very important.

But in a codependent case, the wife, because of fear and guilt, would be very quick to say "Oh, no, no, no. I don't think I can do that, but thank you."

April O'Leary: What about when the wife has fear about her husband's response – she doesn't want to deal with it, and because of that, she waits till the last minute to tell him? Maybe she fears that if she would have told him in the morning, then he would have been mad at her all day, and she would not be able to handle that.

Dr. Michael Woulas: When you have a high level of codependency there is the fear of being disapproved of or rejected, as we talked about previously. So, a person with a high level of codependency is going to do everything possible to avoid those kinds of situations.

April O'Leary:	So, if this situation were to play out in a normal, healthy manner without these fearful and guilty feelings, how would a wife respond to that offer? What would her thought processes and her feelings be that would be appropriate?
Dr. Michael Woulas:	That's a great question. She would have to be able to give herself a little bit of time to think about herself and what she wants and needs. She would consider when the last time was that she went somewhere (for her own well-being), as well as giving thought to her husband and his needs and her children and their needs. So, she would try to strike a balance there, but that's not going to happen if she is unable to focus a little bit more on herself.
April O'Leary:	When you say 'consider her needs,' it seems to me that those who struggle with codependency have an over-focus on others' needs without any focus on our own. So, the other end of the pendulum would be focusing solely on our own needs and saying, "I don't care what everybody else thinks. I am doing this." So, what you are saying is to get right in the middle where you are focusing on you but you are also being considerate of others. Is that what you mean?
Dr. Michael Woulas:	That's exactly it. That's what's called having balance, April.
April O'Leary:	That particular woman might consider whether she likes that show and whether she wanted to go or not. She may decide she doesn't want to go because she is not interested, but if she decides that this is something she really wants to do then she might just make that decision and call her husband. If this is the case: What should she say?
Dr. Michael Woulas:	Just be honest and truthful that she has gotten a phone call from Debbie who has offered tickets, and she would like to go.

April O'Leary:	And then if there is no real reason why she is not able to go, she can go and allow everyone else to feel however they decide to feel about it even if her husband is making her feel guilty or the kids are crying, she able to handle that.
Dr. Michael Woulas:	If she doesn't have a lot of codependency, yes.
April O'Leary:	Right. The responses might not change, but she is able to handle it in a way that still allows her to go and have a good time.
Dr. Michael Woulas:	Yes.
April O'Leary:	Thank you, Dr. Woulas, for all of your insight and knowledge about overcoming fear and guilt with great examples, too.
	This concludes Lesson 3. Please complete the activity to see if fear and guilt are a problem for you.

Lesson 3 Activity

Now that you have completed Lesson 3 please answer the following questions:

Where do guilt and fear come from?

Give one example of guilt that is appropriate and based on rational thinking.

Give one example of guilt that is inappropriate and based on irrational thinking.

Give one example of fear that is appropriate and based on rational thinking.

Give one example of fear that is inappropriate and based on irrational thinking.

Bonus: What role does thought have in emotion? How can you differentiate between irrational and rational thoughts?

Lesson 3 Summary

We hope that you have learned where fear and guilt come from and how to recognize it in your own thought patterns. Overcoming fear and guilt may take some time as you begin to differentiate rational, realistic thinking from irrational and unrealistic thought processes. However, as you start to identify these thinking patterns they will become easier to identify.

To conclude please write your answers to the following questions:

1. What was most important to you this lesson? Why?

2. Explain how thinking and emotion are related.

3. How do you plan to reduce the frequency of fear and guilt that you experience? (Tip: Consider whether your fearful and guilty feelings are based on rational or irrational thoughts.)

Lesson 4:

How I Overcame Guilt –
A Personal Story

Lesson 4 Overview

In this lesson you will listen to April tell her personal story of how she overcame guilt and fear. Hopefully, through these real-life examples, you will be able to see guilt and fear more clearly in your own life. This will help you to distinguish between guilt and fear, which is normal and appropriate, and what is unhealthy and inappropriate.

By the end of this lesson you will be able to identify ways in which you are allowing unhealthy guilt and fear into your own life and relationships and consider how you might change these patterns.

Please write your answers to the following questions:

Write your understanding of where emotions, such as fear and guilt, come from. (Tip: How do thoughts and perceptions relate to emotions?)

Give one example of a time when you felt guilt or fear in your own life.

Can you identify the specific thoughts and perceptions that triggered your emotions?

Lesson 4

How I Overcame Guilt – A Personal Story

April O'Leary:

Welcome to Lesson 4 of *Focus on You*. Today I'll be sharing my personal story with you about how I was able to overcome unhealthy guilt in my own life. I am April O'Leary and I'm here again with Dr. Michael Woulas.

Hi, Dr. Woulas.

Dr. Michael Woulas:

Hi, April.

April O'Leary:

In Lesson 3, if you recall, we talked about overcoming fear and guilt. You shared with us a very clear analogy of healthy and unhealthy fear with regards to feeling fear when crossing a road when a truck is coming and also feeling fear to cross that same road when a truck is not coming. I think that was a very good way to clarify that fear comes from our thoughts and perceptions of situations. Then we talked about healthy and unhealthy forms of guilt and discussed how guilt might show up in a codependent relationship.

Today I would like to share with you my story of overcoming fear and guilt which I think will give a deeper connection for many who may be struggling with unhealthy guilt and fear.

So, go ahead, ask any questions you would like to ask, Dr. Woulas. I will try to answer as honestly as possible.

Dr. Michael Woulas:

Okay. April, first I want to thank you for your willingness to follow up the previous lesson with your own experience. There is nothing better for a listener than to participate in an actual experience rather than some hypothetical stories. So, this is the real thing. I think you are willing to share some details and give some pretty good examples of what it's like to have guilt, or experience guilt, in your marital and family relationships and how you have been able to overcome it.

So, how does this story actually begin, April?

April O'Leary: Alright. I grew up in an environment where it was always appropriate to think about others first, which as we discussed is the way many people, especially girls are taught to behave. I was taught a lot through religion about sacrificing yourself and being a sensitive and giving person, it was easy for me to adopt this mentality, which is not harmful, to a degree. I was always a part of service organizations and volunteered my time to those in need, and I never really saw anything wrong with that. But as a single woman I was still able to make time for myself and do the things I wanted to do too. Where this pattern really started taking toll is when I got married and began having children.

Suddenly, I was a young mother, with three children under the age of five, and I just did what I knew to do up to that point in my life, serve others. So, I made it my job to make sure everyone else was happy, from doing all the household work, to arranging kids' activities and school schedule, cleaning, cooking, and holding a job too and I didn't ask anyone to help me, because my main thought was that I needed to be of service to others and that it was not okay to need help or to admit that I couldn't handle it all. It was exhausting. So, that's how I started into this pattern of fear and guilt.

Dr. Michael Woulas: So, basically, you are describing a learning experience, aren't you? That you developed a way of functioning as a wife and as a mother based on what you learned from past experiences.

45

April O'Leary:	Yes. There are probably men who have these similar patterns, but I think it's very common for women. Especially culturally, around the world, it is common for women to be secondary to men or to defer to their needs above their own. Also, when you are in that role of mother, you have the feeling that it is your job to take care of everyone else. That's your job, and you don't really question it – you just do it because that's what you think you are supposed to do.
Dr. Michael Woulas:	And to a degree there is really nothing wrong with that, is there?
April O'Leary:	No, there isn't. However, I became so focused on others, and I had no focus on me. So, if I wasn't happy, rather than being able to validate that I ignored it. If someone else was unhappy, I couldn't see that as their problem, I took it personally. I felt that it was my job to make them happy. If someone in my family, or one of my friends was unhappy I would ask them if I did something wrong, and I would feel that I was somehow responsible.
Dr. Michael Woulas:	What you are basically saying is, "I am taking responsibility for the way you are feeling and acting right now." And because you think you have done something wrong you probably are going to feel some guilt.
April O'Leary:	Exactly. That was how it started. I was unable to see that others are responsible for their own feelings and thought I was the one responsible, so when others didn't feel good, I felt like I had done something wrong and I felt guilty about it. This is unhealthy guilt, which as you described is being afraid to cross the street when there really is no truck coming. The more I felt that I was responsible for someone else's feelings the more guilty felt. As life gets busier and more stressful within a family, often the mom tries to lighten the load for

46

everyone else and finds her load is just too heavy to bear. That is what I did. I wanted to make sure everyone else had a calm, easy and relaxed life, but I was drowning. I didn't want to put anyone else out, so I set my needs aside completely. Like Dr. Woulas described in the previous lesson I couldn't see that the responses of the kids crying when I left would be a normal response, so I was not able to handle that and therefore did not do much for me to avoid those situations.

Dr. Michael Woulas: And that becomes a vicious circle, April, doesn't it?

April O'Leary: It does. I was lost. Luckily I had a strong marriage, and, thankfully, through some great therapy I was able to get help and correct my thinking. But at that time I was not doing things that I wanted to do because I was afraid that I would be adding more stress to our already stressful life. I didn't see my needs as important and on top of that I felt guilty for not being the happy woman I wanted to be.

Dr. Michael Woulas: So if you considered doing something for yourself you were telling yourself, "I am doing something wrong." Therefore you are going to feel guilt, when in reality you really hadn't done anything wrong at all. It was just your perception, your thought, that you did something wrong that produced your guilt.

April O'Leary: When my children were toddlers, I was an at-home mother, and I belonged to a MOMS Club. They hosted a mom's night out once a month and it was one night I dreaded. I wanted to go, but I felt selfish that I was taking a night off from childcare. I would dread bringing up the topic of going to the night out with my husband, and would leave it to the last minute. Sometimes I would not go at all because I felt too much guilt over going out for the night. If I did decide to go, I would take care of everyone else first. I would make their dinner, give the kids their baths, clean up the dishes, and get everyone set up so that my night off, if you can call that a night off, would not inconvenience anyone else. You see, that is how I thought that it was my job to meet everyone else's needs first, and mine last. I often was so tired by the time I got out, or so frazzled, I had a hard time enjoying myself. It just felt like more to do, rather than a time to have fun with friends without kids.

Dr. Michael Woulas: So you were feeling guilty about going out with friends one night a month. Is that right?

April O'Leary: Right. Feeling like I did something wrong by taking a night off. I also felt guilty spending money on myself too, so I would make sure to order something cheap or I'd eat first with my family at home and just get a dessert. So, that's a silly example, but hopefully you can see that if you are trying to make an effort to take care of yourself, that wouldn't be wrong.

Dr. Michael Woulas: There is no way that that's wrong, and there is nothing that indicates you have done anything wrong. Maybe you don't even realize that you are putting everyone else first. So, how do you move past that? What do you say to yourself?

April O'Leary: I personally wasn't able to move past that until I got so far entrenched in this way of thinking that I was consistently angry, frustrated and resentful. This led me to seek emotional support from an old friend which crossed the line into an emotional affair. At that point I realized I needed help and that the patterns I had created for myself in my marriage were not working. Sometimes it takes those types of moments to realize that we have to make a change. So, I realized that by putting everyone else first I was not only feeling lost, but I was feeling guilty and fearful too. I had to start somewhere by changing something and that meant I had to start changing my own thinking around and start focusing less on others and more on my needs. Once I started my healing process, I can remember going to dinner with a friend and knowing that it was ok to do, but the feelings of guilt persisted. For a while I had to take action and continue doing something different, making decisions that supported my needs, and over time those guilty feelings started to subside. It's like learning to ride a bike – you really have to concentrate on what you are doing at first, and then it becomes second nature.

Dr. Michael Woulas: Exactly. You have to keep doing things, even when it's new. You may be uncomfortable with starting the process of focusing a little more on yourself, but you have to do it, and deal with the guilt that seems to follow with it.

April O'Leary: That was what I did. As I started to take action and make decisions that were more focused on me, my feelings of guilt and anger and fear started to subside. I love to talk about practical strategies, like we did in Lesson 2, when we talked about setting boundaries. So I'd like to share a practical strategy I used at that time to overcome some of my unhealthy guilt and fear. I would ask myself if what I wanted to do seemed realistic and reasonable. For example, "Is it realistic that an at-home mother might want a night off?" or "Is it reasonable that I might want to go get a pedicure once in a while?" I used to feel guilty about buying anything for myself, so when I was in need of something I would ask myself, "Is it reasonable to buy 3 new shirts?" Before I learned this strategy I would feel immense guilt in buying things for myself, but when I did so, I would take the tags off and hide them in the closet and throw away any evidence that I had done anything for me…because I thought it was wrong. So I had to stop with that type of misperception that you were talking about earlier and realize there was nothing wrong with what I was doing. So, little by little I would test my progress. I would not hide the evidence and I would lay the shirts out on the bed. I might still feel guilty that I bought them, but I did it to force myself outside of the comfort zone, to test that boundary and say, "Hey, look at the shirts that I bought today. Do you like them?"

Dr. Michael Woulas:	Then you found out that basically the world didn't come to an end.
April O'Leary:	Exactly.
Dr. Michael Woulas:	That helps, doesn't it?
April O'Leary:	It does help. So, it was baby steps. It was little things. But I can say that when the shirts were lying out on the bed, I was tempted to hide them again. So, feelings of fear would still rise up, telling me I had done something wrong, that I wasn't worth it, that my needs didn't matter, etc. All these fearful thoughts had to run their course, and I had to stick with the program and retrain my thoughts to focus on me a little more. Despite these lingering thoughts, I recognized them as perceiving a truck in the road when there wasn't one there. I was able to see that what I was doing was realistic, and reasonable, and that there was nothing wrong with taking care of me.
Dr. Michael Woulas:	Well, obviously, your marriage was able to handle your change and your attempts at correcting some of these things that you know were unhealthy and detrimental to you personally. What about a situation, April, where a partner is not so accommodating? What would you suggest in that case? I can see some situations where it might not be so easy to go ahead and do these things.
April O'Leary:	For me personally, it wasn't a smooth transition at first. I would say that making changes, even healthy changes, to a relationship takes time and that it is important to recognize that there may be an adjustment period in your life where things may actually get worse before they got better as the balance is readjusting. Just because this happens does not mean you are doing something wrong.

Would you say that's something normal that you see happening in your practice?

Dr. Michael Woulas: Oh, absolutely! And again, this is real. This is not some made-up story that you are sharing. This is real life. And this happens all the time. This is very common in many relationships.

What else comes to mind? What else would you like to share that a partner listening could do to help with that process?

April O'Leary: My advice or recommendation is to persist in taking care of you. The other person might not be so malleable and willing to change in the short run, but if the pattern is not working, someone has to be the catalyst for change and the only person you have control over is you...so start there.

Dr. Michael Woulas: In other words, don't give up even though it may be very difficult. You just touched upon a very important issue that has to do with change, and that's when one person initiates change from a pattern that's been there forever, that change will ultimately create change in the patterns. In other words, the other person has to change in some way to maintain the relationship. So, by persisting in your beliefs and your actions, you will ultimately produce change in your partner without that person even making any conscious effort to do that.

April O'Leary: And as you become more at-ease, more confident, and happier and you understand that what you are doing is realistic, your partner will have to accept it. Remember as you go through this process to ask yourself, "Is it realistic?" – whatever it is that you are struggling with – getting help around the house, going out with friends, buying things for yourself. Anything that you might have felt guilty about in

51

the past, but is normal, healthy and appropriate behavior. This technique will help you move past unhealthy guilt and fear that is trying to inhibit you from meeting your own needs first.

Dr. Michael Woulas: So, you are saying be reasonable, be rational and be realistic.

April O'Leary: Yes, and that will help you decide whether there is really a truck there or whether you just think there is.

Dr. Michael Woulas: Again, none of this is going to happen if you are not focusing a little bit more on yourself and a little less on everybody else to create a more healthy balance for yourself and those around you.

April O'Leary: I think that covers it for our lesson today about how I overcame guilt. Thank goodness I did, because it's no way to live. Once you see that taking care of you and putting the focus back on you really does bring a new sense of freedom and a zest and love for life, it will allow you to enjoy life more. So, I would encourage you to persist in it, and as Dr. Woulas shared with us, as you make those changes it will force the other person to adapt over time. So, don't give up.

Please proceed to the Lesson 4 activity. We have provided different scenarios that ask the question "Is it reasonable?" You have to decide whether or not what is presented is reasonable. This concludes Lesson 4.

Lesson 4 Activity

In this lesson you heard a personal account of unhealthy guilt and fear. Now it's your turn to identify unhealthy patterns stemming from your guilt and fear.

Now that you have completed Lesson 4 please answer the following questions:

Describe below a difficult situation you recently experienced with a significant other.

Now see if you can identify the thoughts and perceptions you had in that situation. Write them below.

Identify the emotions you experienced stemming from those thoughts. Write them below.

Now be aware that your responses came from 1) the situation, then 2) the perception, then 3) the emotion. How does that affect your ability to make healthy changes in the future? Tip: Focus on your own thoughts and perceptions and notice whether they are realistic and reasonable.

Lesson 4 Summary

Listening to a personal story of overcoming guilt and fear can be helpful. You should now be able to see it more clearly in your own life. This will allow you to distinguish between guilt and fear that is normal and appropriate versus what is unhealthy and inappropriate.

We hope that you have been able to identify ways in which you are allowing unhealthy guilt and fear into your own life and relationships. Now you have the tools you need to overcome these negative interpersonal patterns.

To conclude please write you answer to the following question:

1. What was most important to you this lesson and why?

2. Give two specific examples of how you have allowed guilt and fear to interfere with your ability to focus on your own needs.

3. How will you handle these emotions differently in the future? Tip: Focus on you. Remember balance is healthy.

Lesson 5:

Other Causes of Codependency

Lesson 5 Overview

In Lesson 5 you will learn that there are experiences other than alcoholism and drug addiction that contribute to the development of codependency such as sexual, physical and verbal abuse and various other non-substance addictions like being a workaholic. Each one of these experiences can contribute in varying degrees to your ability to focus on yourself and your needs. Achieving a healthy balance in personal relationships also becomes very difficult as a result of these traumatic events mentioned above.

You will learn more about the root causes of codependency, and you will understand where your patterns came from more clearly. If the codependent traits you currently experience, in conjunction with your past, seem to be too difficult to face on your own, we would advise you to seek professional help. Don't be discouraged, these are correctable patterns. Many people have overcome these issues and you can too!

Please write your answers to the following questions:

What kinds of physical or emotional traumas have you been exposed to?

When did they occur in your life span, and who was involved?

Approximately how long and how frequently were you exposed to these traumatic events?

Lesson 5

Other Causes of Codependency

April O'Leary:

Welcome back to Lesson 5. Today, we are going to be talking about other causes of codependency. I am April O'Leary here with Dr. Michael Woulas.

Good afternoon, Dr. Woulas.

Dr. Michael Woulas:

Hi! Good afternoon, April.

April O'Leary:

Today we are going to be covering the other causes of codependency. You may be listening to this and be thinking, "I don't have a husband who is an alcoholic or parents that were" or "I haven't dealt with substance abuse or anything like that," and you may be wondering – even though you are identifying with some of these patterns – how you might have begun adopting these codependent patterns. Today we want you to know that addiction is not the only way that it can happen.

Dr. Woulas is going to take us through some of the other common causes of codependency, and maybe you might be able to see yourself in them or understand it a little bit better.

Dr. Woulas, please tell us what other things can happen so that someone gets these codependent patterns.

Dr. Michael Woulas:

Sure. April, as a quick recap of the last lesson in which you shared your personal story, it was clear that most of the personality traits or issues that made it difficult for you to actually focus on yourself and be able to create a healthy

58

balance for yourself came primarily from learning experiences and being around others who had codependent traits.

Now, there are clearly other reasons why people become codependent, and they have to do with some of the following experiences. For example, people who have been exposed to abuse – and that could be in many different forms: verbal, physical, sexual or a combination of any of those three – would experience emotional trauma that result in traits and personality conditions that make it difficult to focus on themselves.

April O'Leary:
So someone who has experienced even mild forms of abuse over time – can form these patterns of taking the focus off of them and that they may be struggling with the fear and guilt and that surrounds or is a part of the codependent pattern.

Dr. Michael Woulas:
Exactly. Let's take, for example, sexual abuse. Now, we know today, April, that it's widespread and a lot of kids are sexually abused. Unfortunately, it's not an uncommon event or experience. Now, one experience of sexual abuse is traumatic enough to affect that victim for the rest of their lives, and this is the reason why society takes sexual abuse so seriously.

April O'Leary:
For someone who may be listening right now who may be thinking, "Gosh! That happened to me. I had one incident I can remember, and I remember it happened on this day." This might be a light bulb going on. Is that what you are saying?

Dr. Michael Woulas:
Yeah, exactly. One experience is all it takes to develop fear, to develop guilt, to have difficulties with intimacy and to have sexual problems in a marriage, so forth and so on. There is a

long list of problems that evolve as a result of one traumatic experience that came from a sexual assault of some kind.

April O'Leary:	Let's talk about a teenager who is dating in high school, and she has a boyfriend who is verbally abusive. How might that affect her?
Dr. Michael Woulas:	Now we are going from the sexual abuse to verbal abuse. Verbal abuse is serious, but it's not nearly as serious in terms of effects on person as a sexual assault. Verbal abuse is basically an experience that a person has where words have been said that have been hurtful; they have been damaging either through put-downs or abusive language. Cursing at a person and belittling them in some form would be considered verbal abuse, and those kinds of experiences would clearly result in difficulties later on with focusing on yourself and taking care of yourself. Interestingly, that's generally the pattern.
April O'Leary:	That would mean that you are focusing on constantly taking care of others because of the patterns that develop from the abuse.
Dr. Michael Woulas:	Yeah, look at what happens in verbal abuse. Like I said, it usually takes the form of hurting another person and putting them down verbally. So, that person has been subjected to rejection and hurt. Which becomes traumatic for them, and as a result of that, they can develop most of the codependent personality traits that we have talked about in the other lessons.
April O'Leary:	Let's take the example of someone who was in a past relationship that was verbally abusive. Maybe they left that relationship, and they are now with somebody else who is not verbally abusive. Might they still have those patterns?

Dr. Michael Woulas:	Certainly they are going to carry fear and guilt. Now, again, this depends on the severity, and when we talk about those things, April, we always have to keep in mind that there are different classifications of codependency and emotional problems of fear and guilt – they are either mild, moderate or severe depending upon the seriousness of the trauma. So, somebody who has had maybe a verbally abusive relationship during adolescence for a few weeks may not experience as much trauma and may carry a little bit of fear and guilt and some of the other traits, but obviously that's not going to last for a long time, as long as the abuse doesn't continue.
April O'Leary:	Going back to the self-assessment in Lesson 1 what you are referring to now is that there are different levels. So, wherever your answers fell within those brackets will show you where the severity of the codependency lies, right?
Dr. Michael Woulas:	Yes and this is pretty much common sense, April. A person who has been exposed to years, beginning in childhood, in a home where one or both parents had problems with anger and their temper, and during those episodes of anger and rage, a lot of hurtful things were said, obviously, that's going to result in some pretty severe and chronic difficulties with fear, guilt and many of the codependent traits that we have talked about, like being unable to focus on yourself, thinking that you are responsible for other people's feelings, not knowing how to like yourself and looking for approval and recognition from others.
April O'Leary:	Let's touch on that again, because I think that's an important point you just made: that you are not responsible for other's feelings.
Dr. Michael Woulas:	When a person has been emotionally or physically or sexually abused, they begin to take responsibility for what happened. So, it is very common to think that you have had some

responsibility in that person treating you in that way and therefore have thoughts that say, "I have done something wrong."

April O'Leary:

That's where it is important to realize that you didn't do anything wrong. That would be equivalent to thinking that there is a truck coming but it really isn't. Because you are accepting those thoughts that you have done something wrong, when you didn't, that's where all the fear and guilt are coming from. You think that it was your fault, not realizing it wasn't.

Dr. Michael Woulas:

Yes, it's traumatic. These experiences that a person goes through affect their thinking. Just think of soldiers in combat. Most people have heard of post-traumatic stress syndrome because it's all over the media. Soldiers who have been exposed to serious gory combat situations come back with post-traumatic stress syndrome. Basically that all begins with those experiences affecting the way the soldier thinks – very negatively – which produces a lot of the symptoms that are connected with post-traumatic stress disorder.

April O'Leary:

So, how does the example of the soldier correlate with someone who has experienced some of these abuses you are talking about?

Dr. Michael Woulas:

Well, it's trauma, April.

April O'Leary:

So, the trauma from those abuse scenarios would be similar.

Dr. Michael Woulas:

Exactly. Trauma from a traumatic experience, depending upon the seriousness of the trauma, affects the way a person thinks. So, milder forms of abuse are going to alter a person's thinking. It won't alter it nearly as badly as being exposed to a much more severe or serious type of abuse which will create a lot of thinking that's not realistic, that's irrational and not logical.

In the case of abuse, the thinking and perception – "this was horrendous," "something bad is happening," "my life may be in danger" – all of that kind of thinking is going to be appropriate for that situation, but once that is over, they carry those thoughts with them, and those thoughts creep into different areas of their lives that are totally separate from the traumatic experience.

April O'Leary: That makes a lot of sense. Somebody who is in the moment, in that experience, where something serious is happening – those thought patterns are appropriate. However, once that abuse is over, if they continue with those same thought patterns, that's what creates the problems.

Dr. Michael Woulas: Exactly. And keep in mind that all it can take is one traumatic experience to have that kind of effect. So, you can see that codependency, and all the associated traits, make it hard for a person to be able to focus on themselves and take care of themselves in a healthy way. It can come from other sources besides just having some exposure to somebody with an addiction or being in a family that has some family member with codependent traits.

So, basically, what we are saying is just keep in mind that being exposed to trauma which can come in various forms or experiences like verbal abuse, physical abuse and sexual abuse, which are all very common out there today to some degree, set the stage for codependency.

April O'Leary: If someone is listening right now, what do you recommend they do?

Dr. Michael Woulas:	Well, you have to become aware and see how you are feeling generally each day of your life. You have to ask yourself questions like, "Am I an overly anxious person?" "Do I worry too much?" "Do I seem depressed too often?" "Am I having difficulties in relationships with my spouse and family?" "Has my job been affected by the way I feel?"
April O'Leary:	That is good advice. So, what we are trying to show is that it's not simply from addiction only. There are a lot of other ways and experiences that people may face that can create these patterns.
Dr. Michael Woulas:	And they may not even be aware that those are the core reasons why they are having some of these difficulties in their lives today, like I just mentioned.
April O'Leary:	So how does understanding help with the process of healing? What should be the one takeaway that someone comes away with after Lesson 5?
Dr. Michael Woulas:	You always need to know what is wrong with something before you fix it. The first step in healing or correcting any problem is finding out the root cause of the problem. So, if somebody leaves this lesson with that 'aha' moment of "there's the reason," then they have just begun the process of correcting and healing themselves from it. From that point it's a matter of deciding how serious these effects have been. Sometimes self-help is just being aware that you have become a little too negative in life and in your thinking, and when you start paying more attention to correcting it, that can make a big difference.
	If it is more serious and chronic, as in a long history of anxiety, depression or substance abuse, that says that there may be a need for a more professional help.

April O'Leary: Great. These are all good insights, and I think that those of you who are listening maybe had a few of those 'aha' moments and said, "Now I understand; now this makes sense to me." And if that's what you are feeling right now, that's great, because as Dr. Woulas just said, identifying and understanding 'why' is the beginning of healing.

Thank you, Dr. Woulas, for your insights. Congratulations on making it through Lesson 5. Just by doing that you are showing that you are starting to put the focus back on to you. Please finish off the lesson by completing the activity provided.

Lesson 5 Activity

With a greater understanding of your past and with increased awareness of the root causes of codependency, it's your turn to do a self-assessment.

Rate yourself on the scale below in the following manner: 1 being mild to 10 being severe codependency. Take into consideration the self-assessment in Lesson 1 and the questions you answered in the introduction to Lesson 5.

Mild				Moderate				Severe	
1	2	3	4	5	6	7	8	9	10

Explain the basis of your assessment in detail below.

Lesson 5 Summary

Through this lesson we hope that you have learned that there are experiences other than alcoholism and drug addiction that contribute to the development of codependency such as sexual, physical and verbal abuse, and various other non-substance addictions like being a workaholic. Each of these experiences can contribute in varying degrees on your ability to focus on yourself and your needs. Achieving a healthy balance in personal relationships also becomes very difficult as a result of these traumatic events.

Now that you have learned about the root causes of codependency, you should understand where your patterns came from more clearly. If the codependent traits you currently experience, in conjunction with your past, seem to be too difficult to face on your own, we advise you to seek professional help. Don't be discouraged; these are correctable patterns. Many people have overcome these same issues, and you can, too!

To conclude please write your answers to the following questions:

1. What was most important to you in this lesson? Why?

2. What specifically did you identify with, and how did it make you feel?

3. What are the next steps you feel you need to take in order to deal with those feelings?

Lesson 6:

Creating Happiness Begins with You!

Lesson 6 Overview

In this lesson you will hear about the importance of taking responsibility for your own happiness. Although joy can come from relating to others, you are ultimately responsible for your own emotions.

We hope that you will learn to identify the reasons for which you are unhappy. Trying overly hard to please others will not result in your own personal joy. That joy comes from an internal process involving your thoughts and feelings.

The activity provided will help you recognize the myths associated with where happiness originates and who is actually responsible for your joy. The activity will also help you find balance between thinking of others versus thinking of yourself and how that affects your own happiness.

Please answer the following questions before beginning the lesson:

List some of the reasons why you believe you are unhappy.

Where do you think happiness comes from?

What do you think you can do to become a happier person?

Lesson 6

Creating Happiness Begins with You!

April O'Leary: Welcome back to *Focus on You* this is Lesson 6. This is April O'Leary here again with Dr. Woulas. Today, we are going to learn that 'Creating Happiness Begins with You.'

Welcome, Dr. Woulas.

Dr. Michael Woulas: Hi, April.

April O'Leary: We have been talking a lot about *focusing on you*, and today we are going to find out where happiness comes from and how we can go about achieving happiness.

Dr. Michael Woulas: This is a very important lesson to conclude our series with because the more you can release the guilt and fear that we have covered in Lessons 1-5 the more you can take this next step to creating happiness in your life. So, maybe you could share a little bit about how you have found happiness to begin with you.

April O'Leary: Sure. We talked over the course of these classes about letting go of focusing on everybody else, starting to take care of ourselves and getting over the idea that that's selfish – that everybody else needs to come first –and getting over the feelings of fear and guilt that are associated with putting ourselves first. So, now we are going to talk a little bit further about creating happiness and how it begins with us.

In my own life as I started to do what I felt was reasonable and as started to let go of those feelings of fear and guilt, I

70

was able to let go of the idea that it's my job to control someone else's feelings about my decisions that are reasonable and realistic. As we talked about in earlier lessons, putting the focus back on me was refreshing and I was able to be happy about doing things that I felt realistic and reasonable. I was able to be happy because I was not worried about how others would respond so much and I did not take personal responsibility for their responses anymore.

So, you see, as we start to let go of the idea that we have any control over how other people choose to think and behave and act, and we start focusing on ourselves and making decisions that make us happy that are also reasonable and realistic, then we can truly begin to be happy.

Dr. Michael Woulas: Now, April, you are giving some very specific instruction and direction on what it means to actually make yourself happy. I guess what it comes right down to, based on what you are saying, is freeing yourself of fear and guilt; that's essential. Many people don't understand what it means to let go of something like this. So, in fact, letting go actually means to stop thinking things that don't make sense, that aren't realistic or rational; and once you do that, then you have actually let go the unrealistic thoughts that create the fear and guilt you are feeling.

April O'Leary: That's exactly it. To me, part of that was realizing that it was not my job to make someone else happy. The focus of our whole series, *Focus on You*, can be boiled down to this: The more I focus on others, the more unhappy I will be, because when I do, I am putting all my power and all my happiness in a basket that I have no control over, because I can't choose how someone else is going respond, how they are going to act or how their emotions are going to be in that moment. But I can choose my thoughts, and I can choose my feelings. So, I focus on being realistic and being reasonable and asking myself questions like, "What works for me?" "What do I want to do?" and then, when I can answer those questions and take action on the answers, I can be happy.

Dr. Michael Woulas: Exactly. So, another important step along the way of creating your own happiness and joy in life is to not only recognize that you have thoughts and perceptions of people and relationships that aren't realistic, that need to be changed, but you also need to start paying a little more attention to yourself and asking yourself questions like, "Is this okay with me, or is it not okay?" "What are some of the things that I like in life that I might not be doing today?" So, it's that focus on yourself that is a very important step in creating happiness.

April O'Leary: That's very true and I think that, again, this fear that comes up sometimes is the idea that "If I am focusing on myself then I am going to be selfish or self-focused," But if you think of a pendulum on one side is complete focus on others, denying our own needs, and on the other side is complete self-focus, doing whatever you want with no regard for others. We are trying to strike a balance here though. So many of us have gotten so far over on the focus on others side that it is necessary to swing the pendulum a little bit and point ourselves back to the center.

Dr. Michael Woulas: I think we have to keep reiterating, April, that focusing on ourselves is not meant to imply that we totally ignore the needs and feelings and thoughts of other people. It's just creating more of a balance between others and ourselves.

April O'Leary: Yes and as we discussed, communication is a big part of that — starting to communicate once we know what our needs are. Sometimes we don't even know what the needs are, what we might want, but then once we figure out what we want or what makes us happy, we have to be able to communicate in a way that is realistic and takes into consideration the needs of others as well.

Dr. Michael Woulas: Now you have touched on a third step. So, the first step was try to work on your perceptions, change those that are not realistic to more realistic thinking; then begin to focus a little bit more on yourself and what you think, feel and need; and then number three is to begin to communicate that.

April O'Leary:

I know this is a kind of a fourth point here, but being okay with being the shifting partner is also important. If you are in a marriage or some partnership and something is not working, someone is going to have to be the catalyst for change, and so there is going to be a learning process. When we are finding out what we want, and then we start to communicate about it we have to recognize that the responses that we get from others – such as the kids still crying when we leave to go to the movies with our friends – might not change. And we have to be okay with that because we are establishing a new pattern in which we are meeting our needs to be happy and we know this is a healthy step.

Dr. Michael Woulas:

That's bringing us to an important question which is: Why does trying to make yourself happy often create problems? What would you say about that, April? In other words, when we're taking those three basic steps that we just talked about, a person may find that they experience some problems that they didn't anticipate.

April O'Leary:

There is. When someone decides to make a change in their relationship, the other person is kind of forced to change, too. For example, when a pattern has been established in which partner A is used to the partner B always taking care of them, coddling them and behaving in a certain way, it can be a rough learning process for partner A because they are used to you going to great lengths to make them happy. And we are actually doing them a disservice in this scenario because we are allowing them to rely on us for their happiness. So each person has to shift to the thinking that they are responsible for their own happiness. The more we try to make somebody else happy, the less happy they become. It becomes a vicious cycle because they are not really learning the strategy of making themselves happy.

Dr. Michael Woulas:	I can also see in this process in terms of creating problems that the person who you would have been focusing on too much in the past, would maybe become annoyed with the new aspect to the relationship. Maybe that person would be used to seeing you as a person who doesn't have confidence or self-esteem. Essentially you are putting yourself in a position where you are probably losing some respect as an individual. Would you agree?
April O'Leary:	I can see that being possible. But when you are being rational and being realistic, when you take steps to improve your own life, you have to understand that everyone might not jump right on board with you. It's like having two overweight partners, for example, and one decides "I am tired of being overweight. I am going to start exercising and eating health." That doesn't mean that the other partner, who is sitting there and is still overweight, is going to automatically jump on board and be supportive of their partner and start dieting and exercising with them. They might not be.
Dr. Michael Woulas:	Right. They may never be.
April O'Leary:	But the person who is making the healthy choice has to be okay with their decision regardless of what the partner thinks. The partner might not be so supportive and the healthier partner might expect or think, "Well, maybe they would buy more healthy food at the store so that I wouldn't be so tempted to overeat," but when they come home with bags full of cookies and donuts, and you may feel like they are try to sabotage you. But if you know you are really being realistic you can say, "You know what, I am going to focus on me. I know that this is a healthy choice. It's only going to improve my life. My doctor told me that I need to lose 50 pounds, and I'm going to do it." Then you can stick with the program because you know that you are doing something that's benefiting you, and you are not doing something to harm somebody else. You are simply focusing on what's going to improve you.

Dr. Michael Woulas: Although it would be very nice to have your spouse jump on board with you and begin to work in this way, that may not happen; and again, if you are focusing too much on that person and not enough on you, that could create a problem with you becoming discouraged, not only with yourself, but with the effects on your spouse or your partner. So, I guess what you are saying is to be careful of that, because that's a potential problem.

April O'Leary: Yes and recognizing they are making a realistic decision is the key. They are not doing anything wrong but are making healthy choices based on thoughts such as, "My former eating habits weren't working for me. I have diabetes now. I can hardly walk up a flight of stairs anymore." So they make that rational decision: "I need to do something better for myself." In the end that will make them overall healthier and happier.

On the same parallel is where maybe you have hit a brick wall, and you were taking care of everybody else and you have done everything to make everybody else happy. Then you feel like, "I am lost. I don't know who I am anymore. I don't know what I like. I feel miserable. I am tired of taking care of everybody else." That's the parallel to visiting the doctor and finding out you need to lose 50 pounds. You are realizing that the patterns that you have been working with aren't working for you. So, then you have a decision to make and you can say, "Either I can continue doing what I am doing and get the same thing, or I can choose to focus on me more, do what makes me happy, allow others to think what they will, and do what they will, and not be so concerned about everybody else."

Dr. Michael Woulas: Just trying to create that balance for yourself in each and every relationship that you have, that's important to you. And, April, we are not saying that that other people are responsible for our inability to focus on ourselves. That's not the implication or intention at all. We talked a little bit about that in between lessons, and I think it's very important that we finish up on this.

April O'Leary:	Right, right. No, it's your own perception and the great thing about that is you can change your perception! It's like the example of the truck. What I just loved about that example is that <u>we</u> are the ones who are standing on the side of the road. It's not somebody else. We are the ones standing there, and we are looking both ways. If we are constantly perceiving this truck that's not there, then we are the ones that have to change our perception. Although we may think others have to change, that is not in our control; you have to make a decision to change. You are the one who is perceiving a truck.
	There are many happy at-home mothers out there who are able to balance their lives well and make time for themselves while getting the help they need. It was my perception of my own job as an at-home mom that made it troublesome for me. I was in the mode of sacrificing myself to a degree that I got angry, resentful and frustrated with the whole thing, but it could just have easily happened to a working mom. It could just have easily happened to a wife and a husband who have no children. It's not the role per se that causes us to become this way; it's where our focus is as an individual. If you can ask yourself, "Who am I focusing on? Am I making decision focusing most of my time and energy on others?" and then ask yourself, "How does it make me feel?" I think those are good questions.
Dr. Michael Woulas:	I think being an at-home mom today has some negative stigma to it. We are basically trying to create an opposite opinion, that a stay-at-home mom is a very important role – not for every single woman or mom – but it is a very important role in society today, and it's hard, when you are that stay-at-home mom, to be able to focus on you and take care of you. So, ultimately, if she learns to do that for herself, she would probably become a better wife and a better mom. Wouldn't you agree?

April O'Leary:	I would definitely agree, and that was one thing that I would mention, that you touched on a little bit earlier, that the more that you input to yourself and do things that make you happy, the more your happiness will affect others because you no longer have to complain and say, "No one's done anything for me lately!" Like that old song, "What Have You Done for Me Lately" – it's like that. That idea is no longer nagging you because you are not living that way anymore. You are doing what makes you happy, and therefore you can just be happy. You can be happy when you are home. You can be happy with your children. You can be happy when you are with your husband because you are not looking to him to make you happy. So, it takes the pressure off of them, too. It's like you are not sitting at home miserable waiting for someone to do something to make you happy because that day might not come. Who knows? Go buy yourself some flowers, right?
Dr. Michael Woulas:	Exactly. And as you learn to do these things and live this way, when the difficult times do come – and it's guaranteed that life is not always going to be filled with joy and happiness each and every day –you will be able to cope. What you are describing in this lesson here is a very important coping strategy.
April O'Leary:	Yes. The whole point of everything that we have talked about here is to know yourself, be okay with what makes you happy and then go about doing the things that make you happy, releasing the ideas that it's selfish and releasing the feelings of fear and guilt. If you can do all that, you will be well on the way to be happy.
Dr. Michael Woulas:	That's hard to disagree with, April. I think you've got me convinced.
April O'Leary:	I will share for the last time here in this course that I was, for a long time, trying to make everybody else happy, and it

didn't work. So, I would encourage any of you out there who are stuck with the idea that focusing on you is selfish or that you are waiting for the romantic idea of "I'll meet my prince charming, and he is going to make me happy, and I am going to make him happy," to realize that it's a backward way of thinking. Maybe you found a partner who you enjoy spending time with, but that doesn't mean that now it is their responsibility to make you happy or your responsibility to make them happy.

Dr. Michael Woulas: That lies within ourselves.

April O'Leary: Exactly.

Dr. Michael Woulas: And that doesn't mean that there is anything wrong with doing something that you know your partner or spouse enjoys. Of course you want to do those things, too. That's just being giving and caring. Again, it always goes back to striking a balance, doesn't it?

April O'Leary: Yes, it does. I want to thank you for all of your great insights, Dr. Woulas, in Lesson 6 here today, and I want to thank you listeners for sticking with us for six lessons. There is an activity to complete, and once you have completed it, if you have further questions to follow up, please feel free to visit either of our websites at hereishelp.net or apriloleary.com. So, congratulations on finishing Focus on You: Your Needs Matter, Too.

Lesson 6 Activity

Now that you have completed Lesson 6 please answer the following questions:

Why does the idea, "It's my job to make you happy, and it's your job to make me happy," create problems?

What are the benefits of creating your own happiness and allowing others to create theirs?

Is it possible for you to think too much about yourself?

After looking at your busy schedule, list a few ways that you can start to take care of you and develop your own happiness.

Lesson 6 Summary

Now that you have completed Lesson 6 you understand the importance of taking responsibility for your own happiness. You also realize that although joy can come from relating to others, you are ultimately responsible for your own emotions.

We hope that you have identified the reasons for which you are unhappy and that you see that trying overly hard to please others will not result in your own personal joy. However, you can create joy in your life though your thoughts and feelings.

To conclude please answer the following questions:

1. What was most important discovery this lesson? Why?

2. How can you apply what you have learned to improve your own joy?

3. What will you avoid doing in the future to help maintain your happiness?

Conclusion

Now that you have completed *Focus on You*: Level 1, we hope that you are recognizing and improving your abilities to effectively take care of yourself. Please retake the WOCAS test and compare your results with what you scored in Lesson 1.

Woulas O'Leary Codependent Assessment Scale (WOCAS)

Please rate yourself on a scale from 0-3 for each of the statements below.

0= Not at all
1= Occasionally
2= Frequently
3= All the time

_____ I depend on others for approval and acceptance.

_____ I frequently go out of my way to please others

_____ I find it hard to accept criticism from others.

_____ I focus on the needs of others more than on my own needs.

_____ I would much rather avoid confrontations than speaking my mind.

_____ I notice that my actions are determined by external events.

_____ It seems like my value as a person comes from how well I do in life.

_____ As long as others are happy around me, I'm happy.

_____ If I am honest with myself, I would say I have too much fear.

_____ I have a goal of fixing those whom I am closest with.

_____ As a child I experienced some emotional, physical or sexual abuse.

_____ I have been physically, verbally or sexually assaulted as an adult.

_____ I grew up in a very critical family.

_____ I noticed that my parents were frequently concerned about what others thought.

_____ As a child I was corrected for trying to please myself first.

_____ I remember being called selfish if I didn't put others first all the time.

81

_____ One or both of my parents tended to be overly negative in their thinking.

_____ If I am honest with myself I have also become too negative in my thinking.

_____ I label others as selfish if they spend time and money on themselves.

_____ Intimacy tends to frighten me.

_____ I find it difficult to accept praise for most of my accomplishments.

_____ I was raised in a family where alcohol and/or drugs were a problem.

_____ I have never really considered the importance of having emotional boundaries.

_____ I find myself frequently making excuses for other peoples' problems.

_____ I generally feel unfulfilled as a person.

_____ There never seems to be enough time for me in a typical day.

_____ People often see me as a 'pushover' or someone who is too easy with others.

_____ There seems to be something wrong with my intimate relationships, but I can't seem to put my finger on it.

_____ I expect people who say they love me to take care of my needs.

_____ One or both of my parents were usually trying to please and make things right with others.

_____ At least one of my grandparents had a history of alcoholism or substance abuse.

_____ One or both of my parents had a bad temper and would lash out at others.

_____ One or both of my parents never seemed to be emotionally available as I was growing up.

_____ My life seems to be passing by and I'm afraid I've missed out on myself.

_____ If I had to do it over again, I would certainly take more time in life for me.

Please turn the page for scoring.

Scoring of Assessments

SCORING: Now that you have completed the assessment it's time to tally up your answers. You may also record your scoring from your first WOCAS assessment on page 11 below too for easy comparison.

SCORING AFTER LESSON 1:

_____ 3's _____ 2's _____1's _____0's

SCORING AFTER LESSON 6:

_____ 3's _____ 2's _____1's _____0's

RESULTS: If you found you scored less 3's and 2's then you did in the beginning of lesson 1 you have improved! Congratulations. Even a slight improvement will gain momentum over time.

SUMMARY: Taking this course has helped you understand the root causes of codependency so that you can more effectively become aware of it in yourself and help others.

You may continue to use this checklist as a guide to help identify your potential codependent personality traits and work towards even greater awareness

Through completing the exercises provided, you have gained a greater understanding of how your thoughts and perceptions affect your emotions. You are also better able to see your thoughts as 'realistic' or 'unrealistic,' which will help you to change your own actions so that you are able to focus on you.

We trust that you have put time and effort into answering all the questions provided, in writing. Please go back over the material and make sure you have done so because they have been specifically designed to take you to a higher level of awareness and interpersonal development.

To wrap everything up we ask that you complete this final writing assignment.

What did you find especially interesting, surprising or enlightening, and how does it relate to you?

What portions of this course do you feel you need further explained or would you like to research further on your own?

How do you plan to implement these ideas in your life, starting today?

Congratulations on completing Level 1 of *Focus on You*. You have:

- Achieved a greater understanding of codependency and the variety of ways in which it can occur.
- Become more aware of healthy and unhealthy relationship patterns.
- Learned where fear and guilt originate and how to effectively deal with them.
- Acquired a higher level of personal satisfaction in your relationships.

For further information you are encouraged to visit us online at hereishelp.net, apriloleary.com and instituteforlifemanagement.com. It's time for focus on you. Remember, your needs matter, too.

About the Authors

Seeing a need for affordable behavioral health care, Dr. Woulas and April have founded the Institute for Life Management, www.instituteforlifemanagement.com, which aims to provide targeted, specific and affordable behavioral health care courses for virtually anyone, anywhere. This unique combining of the clinical and coaching approach is the first of its kind anywhere. This is the first course in the series. Other topic specific courses to follow will focus on anger, addiction, abuse, depression, attention deficit disorder, chronic pain and goal setting and achievement. To submit a comment or question please email april@apriloleary.com.

 Michael J. Woulas, received his M.A. from Assumption College and Ph.D. from St. John's University. He is a licensed psychotherapist with a thirty-year career diagnosing and treating depression and related mood disorders with specialties in the treatment of adult and pediatric attention deficit and hyperactive disorders, chronic pain syndrome and addictions. Dr. Woulas also has osteopathic medical training from Nova Southeastern University, College of Osteopathic Medicine, which augments his skills as a clinician. He is the author of <u>The Ticking Time Bomb: Anger, Rage and Emotional Volatility of Bipolar Disorder, Type II</u> a practical guide to raise public awareness of the causes for today's violence in families and society and has been in private practice in southwest Florida since 1985 where he lives with his wife. For more information visit hereishelp.net.

 April O'Leary received a B.A. in Education from Northeastern Illinois University and a Master Life Coach Certification from Life Coach Universe in Fort Myers, Florida. She is the Founder of the University of Moms, which provides motivation and inspiration for mothers worldwide and is the author of <u>Ride the Wave: Journey to Peaceful Living</u>. She works with women and men to help them balance their busy lives and achieve more peace and happiness through the process of self-care. April lives in Southwest Florida with her husband and three daughters. To get Chapter 1 of Ride the Wave free visit apriloleary.com and if you are a mom, join us free at the uofmoms.com.

Appendix I

Institute for Life Management
Research Initiative

Our current research effort on the treatment of codependency will focus on a new and innovative format for behavioral health and education created by the Institute for Life Management (I.L.M.). The format is conducted independently through a therapist guided e-workbook with pre and post lesson exercises. A hard copy is also available for those who choose not to utilize the e-workbook format. The content of each recorded lesson consists of intensive interview and discussion on the core issues of codependency. This method offers a more autonomous approach to attaining behavioral health.

As part of I.L.M.'s research initiative, participants will self-administer a codependency rating scale (Woulas O'Leary Codependent Assessment Scale) prior to receiving behavioral assistance through the Focus on You series. Results of the pre-lesson rating scale will provide objective measures of codependency levels, before receiving the complete six-lesson series. The WOCAS will also be self-administered upon completion of the series and at the end of a three month follow-up period to help determine longer term effects.

In addition to a self-administered rating scale, I.L.M. Research Initiative will involve ongoing efforts to establish validity and reliability of the WOCAS and the whole virtual approach to behavioral healthcare. For example, each participant will provide an independent evaluator, who has substantial knowledge of their personality traits and adheres to independent evaluator criteria provided by I.L.M. Correlation and variation analyses of self versus independent measures of codependency will be a part of ongoing validational investigations by I.L.M.

Appendix II

3 Month Follow-Up Assessment

Making life changes of any sort takes time. The more you work on being aware of and changing your codependent patterns the more you will find those around you change too. You may also find that others change too, just because you took the first step!

Retake the assessment below and see how your attitudes, feelings and thoughts compare with where you were only 6 short months ago.

Woulas O'Leary Codependent Assessment Scale (WOCAS)

Please rate yourself on a scale from 0-3 for each of the statements below.

0= Not at all
1= Occasionally
2= Frequently
3= All the time

_____ I depend on others for approval and acceptance.

_____ I frequently go out of my way to please others

_____ I find it hard to accept criticism from others.

_____ I focus on the needs of others more than on my own needs.

_____ I would much rather avoid confrontations than speaking my mind.

_____ I notice that my actions are determined by external events.

_____ It seems like my value as a person comes from how well I do in life.

_____ As long as others are happy around me, I'm happy.

_____ If I am honest with myself, I would say I have too much fear.

_____ I have a goal of fixing those whom I am closest with.

_____ As a child I experienced some emotional, physical or sexual abuse.

_____ I have been physically, verbally or sexually assaulted as an adult.

_____ I grew up in a very critical family.

_____ I noticed that my parents were frequently concerned about what others thought.

_____ As a child I was corrected for trying to please myself first.

_____ I remember being called selfish if I didn't put others first all the time.

_____ One or both of my parents tended to be overly negative in their thinking.

_____ If I am honest with myself I have also become too negative in my thinking.

_____ I label others as selfish if they spend time and money on themselves.

_____ Intimacy tends to frighten me.

_____ I find it difficult to accept praise for most of my accomplishments.

_____ I was raised in a family where alcohol and/or drugs were a problem.

_____ I have never really considered the importance of having emotional boundaries.

_____ I find myself frequently making excuses for other peoples' problems.

_____ I generally feel unfulfilled as a person.

_____ There never seems to be enough time for me in a typical day.

_____ People often see me as a 'pushover' or someone who is too easy with others.

_____ There seems to be something wrong with my intimate relationships, but I can't seem to put my finger on it.

_____ I expect people who say they love me to take care of my needs.

_____ One or both of my parents were usually trying to please and make things right with others.

_____ At least one of my grandparents had a history of alcoholism or substance abuse.

_____ One or both of my parents had a bad temper and would lash out at others.

_____ One or both of my parents never seemed to be emotionally available as I was growing up.

_____ My life seems to be passing by and I'm afraid I've missed out on myself.

_____ If I had to do it over again, I would certainly take more time in life for me.

Final Scoring of Assessments

Please record your scores from the previous two assessments below.

SCORING AFTER LESSON 1:

_____ 3's _____ 2's _____1's _____0's

SCORING AFTER LESSON 6:

_____ 3's _____ 2's _____1's _____0's

Now score today's assessment.

SCORING TODAY: Now that you have completed the assessment today it's time to tally up your answers. How many of each did you get?

_____ 3's _____ 2's _____1's _____0's

Now compare your results. How did your rating compare? Write your overall feelings below. What did you notice improved and what do you notice you still need to address?

NOTES

22582357R00055

Made in the USA
Lexington, KY
04 May 2013